The Mad Moonlight

For Iris and Clio

Someday ...

The Mad Moonlight

poems

Louis Jenkins

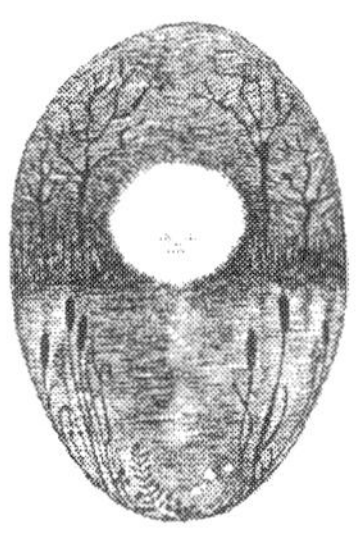

Will o' the Wisp Books

Will o' the Wisp Books
5521 Auto Club Road
Bloomington, Minnesota 55437
www.willothewispbooks.com
Published by Will o' the Wisp Books, 2019
Cover painting by Ann Jenkins, *Party*, 2019
ISBN 978-0-9793128-8-5

Versions of some of these poems originally appeared in the following publications: *Agni, American Poetry Review, Ascent, Barnwood, Black Warrior Review, Borealis, Boston Review, Caprice, Carleton Miscellany, Chariton Review, Cimarron Review, Coda, Columbia, Crazy Horse, Epoch, Everywhere, Gettysburg Review, Great River Review, Hawaii Review, Ironwood, Jublilat, Kenyon Review, Key Satch(el), Knockout, Lake Country Journal, Lake Superior Journal, Lamp In The Spine, Literary Cavalcade, Luna, Manhattan Review, Midwest Quarterly, Milkweed Chronicle, Minnesota English Journal, Ninth Letter, Paragraph, Paris Review, Paterson Literary Review, Poetry Daily, Poetry East, Poetry International, Poetry Now, The Prose Poem: An International Journal, Puerto Del Sol, Parabola, Redactions, Red Weather, Rosebud, Salted in the Shell, Seneca Review, Sentence, Snowy Egret, Speakeasy, Tarpaulin Sky. Terminus, The Sun, Three Candles, Utne, Virginia Quarterly Review, Willow Springs.* or none of the above.

Contents

JANUARY NIGHT 35 BELOW ZERO

When I was a child, I'd burrow
into my covers
pretending to be a rabbit or a fox.
Tonight I will say my prayer
to whatever small creature is moving
in the woods beyond my window.
So fierce in its life.

WINTER EVENING

As we get older we become more alone.
The man and his wife share this gift.
They make love or they quarrel.
They move through the day,
 she on the black squares,
 he on the white.
At night they sit by the fire,
 he reading his book, she knitting.
The fire is agitated.
The wind hoots in the chimney like a child
 blowing in a bottle,
 happily.

SAUNA

Even to step naked
into the January night is a pleasure!
Steam rises from our bodies
and forms high, thin clouds
that go racing past the moon over the lake.

HERE IT IS MARCH

This winter has been going on for eleven years.
It's amazing how one gets concerned
with other things
and the time just goes by.
Here it is March
and now that I've noticed it,
the snow has begun to melt a little.
During the day there's water
running in the street.
It's like a bird singing in a tree
that flies just as you become aware of it.
When you think about it, the world,
cold and hard as it is,
begins to fall apart.

RIVER GORGE

I could carve out
a little place for myself
in 10,000 years or so,
but long before that, life
would have gone all strange
and none of the landmarks
would be familiar.
Like the water,
I'm just passing through,
only I'm not taking
anything with me.

I USED TO

When I got older I used to like
To sit and watch the young women go by,
especially in summer.
That's all I did, watch.
All I could do, really.
Now that I am even older
and my eyesight fails,
I find I can't really see the girls.
Just a blurred memory.

BOREDOM

Nowadays I am seldom bored.
There simply isn't time.
Time passes more quickly as one gets older.
Boredom that once lasted hours is now compacted.
Well, time is relative.
Like that distant relative who used to be me,
plodding home after school in a daydream,
and when he wakes he finds himself standing on the same red ant hill
or running, side aching, breathless,
for miles in the wrong direction with the murderous Willard brothers right behind.

CHEKHOV AND HEISENBERG

I tell my brother-in-law
that we stayed in the hotel where
Chekhov had stayed, in Nice.
He tells me that he once stayed
in the very hotel room that
Werner Heisenberg
had occupied back in 1926.
He thought the hotel was either
in Copenhagen or maybe Leipzig...
But he was uncertain.

APPENDAGE POEM

Every time I look for money
I find a hand in my pocket.

UNIVERSE

Sometimes I think that I am the universe.
Take a look at my bare back;
spots and stars, galaxies,
nebulae, bumps, dark matter, super nova....
But it is all just skin-deep.

SAGES IN SPRING

As soon as the snow melts
the grass begins to grow,
even though the daytime high
is barely above freezing.
May is very like November.
Popple trees produce a faint green
that hangs under the low clouds
like a haze over the valley.
This is how the sages live, no complaints,
no suspicion, no surprise.
If it rains carry an umbrella.
If it's cold wear a jacket.

BIRTHDAY

It's my birthday.
Well, every day is someone's birthday;
 think of that... many people's birthday,
 over 300,000 birthday's every day.
And if today is your birthday,
 remember, nobody gives a shit.
 Just blow out the candles on your cake
 if you are lucky enough to have one.

BREAD UPON THE WATERS

As quickly as that,
in that moment your attention focused
somewhere far out there,
on the bit of sun brightening the surface,
the baby drifted away.
his diaper changed, his bottle filled,
he rides the waves in his basket, like a king,
a bit uncomfortable, and slightly annoyed.

DRIFTWOOD

Driftwood on the beach,
dry and bleached white, white
as a bone you might say, or white as snow.
If an artist (wearing a sweatshirt, blue jeans
and tennis shoes without socks)
came walking along he might,
seeing the possibilities,
pick up this piece of driftwood and take it home.
Not me. I fling it back in the water.

THREE DAY RAIN

It has been raining for three days,
a slow unrelenting rain,
east wind, 43 degrees;
an average day in June.
Everything is soggy and rotting.
Earth worms are drowning.
We have no money, nowhere to go.
The gray goose stands in the yard
with her head under her wing.

RENT FREE

I don't get around very well anymore.
I'm unsteady on my feet.
I can't sit in a canoe anymore.
It hurts my back.
I have trouble sleeping.
My speech is sometimes garbled.
Reading is difficult; no ability to concentrate.
My feet hurt, and I have very low energy.
So these days I live mostly in my head.
You could live there too,
if you need a temporary place to stay.
It's quiet, And there's lots room.

DREAM OF WEALTH

The stars are neither large
 nor very distant.
They are made of delicate glass
imported from Sweden and sold
at a huge profit.

GREEN SNAKE

There is a green snake
moving in and out of our conversation.
Hungry, he eats the dots of the j's and the i's.
We grope blindly for words.

SQUIRREL

The squirrel makes a split-second decision
and acts on it immediately—
headlong across the street
as fast as he can go.
Sure, it's fraught with danger,
sure, there's a car coming,
sure, it's reckless and totally unnecessary,
but the squirrel is committed.
He will stay the course.

PHYSICAL THERAPY

Because I am feeling pretty good today,
I say to my therapist
I think I'll live, at least, five more years.
She says,
"You think?"

THERE IS NO GOD IN HEAVEN

There is no God in heaven
who thinks you are special
the way your mother did.
The earth does not think
you are more special
than any centipede or rat.
The earth is not your mother,
and heaven is not your home.

THE RUNNER

She has long legs and short shorts.
She wears her long blond hair
tied in a neat bun. Each move she makes
is perfect, not too fast, not too slow.
She glides along down the sidewalk,
leaving me breathless,
A block away the sidewalk curves
and she is gone forever.

A QUIET PLACE

I have come to understand my love for you.
I came to you like a man
looking for a quiet place.
A few old houses, the abandoned church,
the river...good fishing.
How I've longed for a place like this!
As soon as I got here, I knew I'd found it.
Tomorrow the set production
and camera crews arrive.
We can begin filming on Monday :
the story of a man looking for a quiet place.

OKLAHOMA

I love this open and rolling prairie,
the vast blue sky
But towns, grain elevators, oil wells, refineries...all
strung together by right-angled roads, seems
altogether the wrong approach.
"Go south two miles, take a right,
take a hard right..."
A tornado doesn't bother.
It blows cross-country rearranging
the debris to suit itself.

DRIP

Water does not want
to be contained.
Silently, secretly,
water feels along
the walls of the pipe for a flaw,
seeks the misthreaded joint,
the faulty faucet.
The drips go orderly,
joyfully into the sink
counting the seconds
of the long night.

HORSE

Having been a passenger
on a horse once or twice,
I understand the rush
to invent the automobile.
Nowadays the horse
is ridden mostly for pleasure,
if you can call it that.
Personally, I prefer to watch horses,
powerful bays and sorrels,
pintos and roans running,
muscles rippling, running across the plains,
over the hills and far away.

ARMCHAIR

I have a large comfortable swivel armchair.
And if I turn it one way
I can see the large-screen tv, and
if I turn the opposite
I can watch the colorful birds
at the feeder.
I suppose it would be more correct to say
that I prefer the birds, but in truth,
I view them both about the same.
Of the things in this poem
I like the armchair best.

POPPLES

Poplar trees aren't popular around here.
Scrap wood, they say, Popples.
But Popples are lovely in fall
when the leaves turn yellow and gold,
or in winter with a new moon
caught in the branches,
and in spring when the rain enhances
the delicate grey-green color of the bark.
I wouldn't mind a view like this
when I come to the bottom
of the slide into old age and senility:
a stand of popples judiciously
framed by the bedroom window
to exclude the junk Chevy
and the trash cans
just to the right.

GREAT GRAY OWL

In fact, he does not care who you are.
He does know that you are not to be trusted.
He fixes you with his yellow-eyed stare,
unapologetic, unafraid.
This is the extent of the wisdom
he has to offer.
Any other questions you may have,
you will have to answer for yourself.

THE WOLF

Where are we going now? I ask
the wolf, as he struggles
to drag my carcass across the snow.
But the wolf does not answer, knowing
it is impolite to speak
with your mouth full.

BAT

There's a bat circling
in the early dark, between
the pine tree, the spruce and the maple.
He seems happy enough gobbling
up hundreds of mosquitoes on each turn around.
But maybe it's Dracula.
You have to think about that.
Maybe Dracula doesn't transform himself
into bat; instead maybe the bat becomes Dracula.
He has to go home soon,
put on his little suit and tie
and wander around the empty castle
muttering to himself in a strange accent.
And later, of course, there will be guests for dinner.

OLD PEOPLE

Some people live too long,
they get foggy and grouchy,
they smell, they sleep and snore,
and pee their pants.
No one really likes old people,
they are in the way. Worst of all
is that they contribute nothing
to the current mass hallucination.

JULY

Temperature in the upper seventies,
a bit of a breeze. Great cumulus clouds pass slowly
through the summer sky
like parade floats.
And the slender grasses gather round you,
pressing forward, with exaggerated deference,
whispering,
eager to catch a glimpse.
It's your party after all.
And it couldn't be more perfect.
Yet there's a nagging thought:
that you don't really deserve all this attention,
and that, come October,
there will be a price to pay.

SUMMER RAIN

Lightening strikes. The clock stops.
The voice on the radio fades.
We sit in the dark living room as in a cave,
without light, without words.

The rain continues to fall all night.
We sleep and drift among roads, houses
and people we have known. I wake and listen,
the sound of rain, the sound of our breathing.
Water rising.

ROCK COLLECTING

I found a really big agate, big as my fist,
half buried in the dirt.
I dug it out using a sharp stick.
I washed off the dirt in the ditch water
and discovered that it wasn't an agate
after all, just an ordinary
reddish-colored rock.
What a relief!
I could drop the rock back in the road.
I could go on with my life.

LITERARY SILLINESS

Jonny Cash sang
I don't care if I do die do die do die.
And Aeneas once said
I don't care for Dido Dido Dido.
As did WS Merwin.

GUILTY

I went down to the Sheriff's Department
and said "I'm here to turn myself in."
"Indeed?" said the deputy.
"And what crime have you committed?"
"I was hoping you could tell me that," I said.

MORNING FOG

I know I'll get back to sleep
when the morning fog comes in,
when the Pacific fleet arrives,
ghost ships from the Coral Sea.
They never cough or shuffle their feet
but I know they're in the room,
great hulking shapes, old
and unpleasant relatives,
the color of the sea, the color of the sky,
gathered around my bed.

WIND FROM THE WEST

It isn't so much because of the desire
for what has been lost,
as it is the loss of desire itself,
that I stand here, on the verge of tears.
like a child, whose big red ball
has washed out to sea,

SKILLET

The skillet has lived a life of service,
worked hard. Forty years or more
at the same job.
The skillet's mouth is always open,
as if it were trying to tell me something
of fire, of darkness and poverty,
but manages only to sputter
platitudes of protestant virtue.
For a moment each morning when I fry eggs,
the skillet opens its large eyes
and stares intently
at me, and at the fork in my hand.

AUGUST EVENING

A cloud of tiny insects hovers just above
the edge of the Lake.
There must be a thousand of them
flying every which way in a sexual frenzy.
It's the world's largest singles bar.
Yet, there is some selection going on,
not just anyone will do.
But it all works out
Mated pairs, drop out of the cloud,
sinking together to the ground.
The weight of it brings them down
while the others continue the dance,
round and round in the warm evening air.

THE TENT

Concave on the windward side,
convex on the lee,
it snaps and strains the ropes.
Green nylon not quite the color of the forest,
it is the flag of nothing in particular,
a banner that proclaims
we will not be here very long,
a modest shelter shedding only
the lightest of rains.
Like home anywhere,
pitched on an unsheltered point,
the tent wants to fly into the air,
heave sideways into the lake.

TEETH

Once you leave the river,
once you start up the long valley
you catch the first glimpse
of mountains snow-capped
sharp white in the distance.
When they see you, smile.

PLEASURE DRIVE

I used to drive most of the time.
But old age caught up to me. Now
my wife does most of the driving.
I've discovered that I like being a passenger.
I have time to look out the window
and at the people,
the trees, the buildings, and the clouds above.
My wife likes it too.
She's honed her skills at moving through traffic,
and she is not opposed to speed now and then.
We strap on our seat belts,
she hums sotto voce to herself.
It's "The Ride of the Valkyries," I think..
And away we go like a bat outta hell.

MAY

Finally, no amount
of kindness or
generosity will help.
In May, the song sparrow
returns. Hidden
in the spring green
his only gift is his song,
all the sweeter because
it isn't meant for you

HEY DIDDLE DIDDLE

I like the high times as much as anyone,
the music and the jokes, flowers, laughter.
I like the night, the wine,
the shadows of trees on the path,
the secret places at the edge of the light,
the breeze soughing in the tall pines.
I also like the sound of the door closing,
the light clicked off.
But now it is nearly two in the morning
and here I am lying awake.
My dish is still out there somewhere,
in the mad moonlight,
last seen in the company of a spoon.

THOUGHTBERRIES

So called because once you spend a
day picking, you will think twice
about ever doing it again.
Thoughtberries are not plentiful,
picking the low stickery bushes
to gather just a handful.
Their scarcity must be part of their appeal
because, really, they aren't all that good.
There are not enough of them in these parts
to make them a commercially viable product,
but then in many parts of the country
they don't grow at all.

YOUTH

One hand holding up
his oversize trousers,
the other clutching a burger,
he races across the street
just ahead of the oncoming traffic.

WHAT IF

I were to die just before
the announcement was made
that I had won the Pulitzer Prize,
or the National Book Award,
or Poet Lariat of the United States,
and the irony of that
were to be entirely lost on me?

PICNIC ON THE SHORE

Shore grass growing
among the big rocks
enduring year after year.
This is the way to live.
A simple life,
the proper arrangement
of a few elements.
But here you are
standing on slippery stone,
trying to balance
a full plate and a cup.
What with the wrappers,
the flies and the wind,
already things
have gotten out of hand.

WITCHES

Young witches

The young witches love to dance
at night in the moonlight, wearing their very
skimpy black dresses.
And the big handsome boys
come down from town.
The girls lead them through the forest,
down the darkened paths. And the boys get turned
around and lost.
Those boys are dumber than sticks, thick as bricks,
and those girls are *wick-ed.*

Old witches

The old witches live in huts deep in the forest.
They know the secret of wolfsbane, snakeroot
plants and herbs.
which are poison and which will make you well.
They make elixirs, potions and poultices,
balm for heartbreak, remorse, disillusionment,
for all the pains of old age and death...
Good luck to you, if you can find them.

KNOCK KNOCK

A large woodpecker is at work
on the wood shingles of my house,
making a terrible racket...
looking for grubs and worms.
He has a different agenda, his own
viewpoint, his own facts,
a separate reality.
I, myself, would never even think of
pecking on a roof.

WEBSITE

An entrepreneurial spider
has built her web between the bars of the railing
at the scenic overlook
in order to catch small insects
blown in on the lake wind.
If you can stick around
she'll tell you all about the difficulties
of owning a small business.

WIND CHIME

Eventually someone will get
sick of this clatter.
This instrument was meant for subtler sounds,
silence and overtones,
only the hint of a breeze,
days in which the phone does not ring
long afternoons that fade into twilight
a single star there in the bell-clear western sky.
But the wind is unrelenting.
It must have been like this long ago,
a single sound over and over
until at last someone sitting alone
became aware of it
and realized what it means to be alive.

TONIGHT THE FULL MOON

Rises above Lake Superior,
All sad and luminous.
and filling me with joy. How many times
have clouds obscured the sky
in the last fifty years?
And how many times have I been lucky
enough to see the moonrise like this?

CONFUSING FALL WARBLERS

This is the way things go,
not high and direct like the geese
with all their honking fanfare
or the eagle riding the rising air,
but like the small birds feeding,
moving from bush to tree to weed,
with what seems like no plan at all,
just one thing leading to another.

TO THE MUSE

All the years I spent waiting for you
to come to me here on this shore,
rehearsing what we would say to one another
and the happiness that would be ours.
Now that I am old, it occurs to me
that you must have come,
but I was too distracted to see you there.

FOLK TALE

Times were tough so we decided
to sell the cow.
I walked the long road into town
leading the cow.
But no one was buying.
On the way home I met a man
who had a horse.
So we swapped. I met others. I swapped
the horse for a pig, the pig for a sheep,
the sheep for a goat, and so on until
I came home with nothing.
But I was born lucky and
the best part of my luck was that
you stood by me
through all the blundering mistakes.
One time I had a windfall.
We were able to buy a new cow...
Which means I'll soon be
on the road again.

THE LAKE

Streets run straight downhill to the water.
The lake brings the city to an end.
It is there, always,
changing the direction of my walks.
Sometimes I go for days
without coming near,
catching only a glimpse through the trees:
a sail, a white speck
turning on the dark blue.
Perhaps someone very old
touched the back of my wrist, lightly,
for only the briefest moment,
or you said something to me.
What was it?

DECEMBER

These winter days are so short, pale,
a lingering twilight
between the long nights,
a scrap of paper shoved under the door
into a dark apartment.
A note, a thinly veiled threat, perhaps
“Only ten shopping days ’til Christmas."
No, something else.
What can be said in such a small space?
Outside, the streetlights are coming on.
"I was able to get here at last.
Sorry to have missed you."

BRIGHTON BEACH WAVES

White-haired but determined,
as if each had a purpose, a private destiny,
someplace to go.
Once the savior walked across the water
to give each wave a hand up.
Perhaps he is returning even now,
but the road to the shore is long, long...
The waves break and fall face forward,
losing touch, losing credibility,
losing all pretense of dignity.

LAKE SUPERIOR

What I like best
are those rocks that
for no apparent reason
stand waist-deep
in the water and refuse
to come into shore.

also by Louis Jenkins

Where Your House Is Now

In the Sun Out of the Wind

Before You Know It

North of the Cities

Nice Fish, a play (with Mark Rylance)

All Tangled Up With the Living

An Almost Human Gesture

Louis Jenkins' poems have been published in a number of literary magazines and anthologies. He has published 12 collections of his poetry. He was awarded two Bush Foundation Fellowships for poetry, a Loft-McKnight fellowship, and was the 2000 George Morrison Award winner. Louis Jenkins has read his poetry on *A Prairie Home Companion* and was a featured poet at the Geraldine R. Dodge Poetry Festival in 1996 and at the Aldeburgh Poetry Festival, Aldeburgh, England in 2007.

The play, *Nice Fish,* based on Jenkins' poems, a collaboration with Mark Rylance, was nominated for an Olivier Award, Best New Comedy in 2017.

Made in the USA
Monee, IL
29 December 2022